Lost Railways of East Sussex
Marie Panter

Kemp Town Station, July 1926.

© Marie Panter, 2013
First published in the United Kingdom, 2013,
by Stenlake Publishing Ltd.
www.stenlake.co.uk
ISBN 9781840335934

Picture Credits

The publishers wish to thank the following for contributing photographs.
Richard Casserley for the front cover, pages 1 , 2, 3, 6, 8, 11, 12, 18, 19, 26, 28, 30, 36, 37, 40, 42, 43, 45, 51, 53; and John Alsop for the inside front cover (both), 4, 5, 7, 9, 10, 13, 14, 15, 16, 17, 20, 21, 22, 23, 24, 25, 27, 29, 31, 32, 33, 34, 35, 38, 39, 41, 44, 46, 47, 48, 49, 50, 52, 54, the inside back cover, and the back cover.

The publishers regret that they cannot supply copies of any pictures featured in this book.

Printed by: Blissetts, Roslin Road, Acton, W3 8DH

Heathfield Station looking south, *c.* 1930.

Introduction

Bordered in the north by Surrey, in the west by Hampshire and in the east by Kent, and measuring a total of 78 miles east to west and 30 miles north to south, Sussex is regarded as one of England's largest counties. In 1888 the county was divided in half for administrative purposes, a revision of the boundary between the two parts being made in 1972 and enacted in 1974. This book covers the railways in East Sussex of that revision.

The first line in Sussex to be opened covered the short distance between Brighton and Shoreham and opened on 12 May 1840. By 1846 trains reached St Leonards in the east. In 1847 the line from Lewes to Newhaven Wharf was made. The main London to Brighton line took three years to construct, employing in that period 3,500 men and 570 horses. The railways within East Sussex were of a varied nature, ranging from standard gauge to tramways, and included a steep-grade railway, a cable railway and even a railway known as 'Daddy Long Legs'!

In the southeast of England three railway companies competed for traffic. The London, Brighton & South Coast Railway monopolised the triangular area created by London, Hastings and Portsmouth. The South Eastern Railway and the London, Chaltham & Dover Railway nearly ruined each other due to their constant competition for the traffic between London and Dover and throughout Kent. With both companies on the verge of bankruptcy, on 1 January 1899 they came together and formed the South Eastern & Chatham Railway, a managing committee comprising directors from both companies. Although effectively merging the two companies, they officially remained separate and receipts were split 59% to the South Eastern Railway and 41% to the London, Chatham & Dover Railway. This was done to avoid the financial costs and risk of a formal merger. Both companies made repeated attempts to invade Brighton territory and tap the traffic from Brighton and Eastbourne.

The decline of the county's railways began during the 1920s due to the increase of motor bus services, which provided more flexible services, and road haulage. In spite of the rationalisation of the Grouping of 1923, which saw the Southern Railway take control of Sussex, passenger numbers continued to fall. The Beeching cuts of the 1960s saw the closure of many lines, but some remain in operation today.

Brighton & Rottingdean Seashore Electric Railway: 'Daddy Long Legs'

Having already successfully built the 'Volks Electric Railway' in Brighton, designer and engineer Magnus Volk decided to build a line which would go through the surf from a pier at Paston Place to one at Rottingdean.

The railway consisted of two parallel 2 feet 8½ inch gauge tracks (or, taking the measurement between the outermost rails, 18 feet gauge). These tracks were laid onto concrete sleepers mortised into bedrock. There was only one car used on the railway, a pier-like construction measuring 45 feet x 22 feet which stood on four legs that were 23 feet high. To move, the car used an electric motor. The official name for the car was 'Pioneer', but due to its appearance it was known as 'Daddy Long Legs'.

The railway was constructed between 1894 and 1896. The official opening was on 28 November 1896 but a storm on the night of 4 December almost destroyed the railway. However, Volks rebuilt it and it reopened in July 1897, and it proved to be very popular. The car was slow moving at high tide and unfortunately Volks never had the finances to improve the electric motor. In 1900 a series of groynes were built near the railway, causing underwater scouring under the sleepers, and the railway was closed for two months for repairs. The council then decided to build a beach protection barrier, which meant that Volks would have to divert the line. With no funds to do so, the railway closed in 1901.

Crowhurst — Bexhill West

Passenger service withdrawn	15 June 1964
Distance	4 ⅓ miles
Company	Crowhurst, Sidley & Bexhill Railway (1897–1905); South Eastern Railway (1905–1922); Southern Railway (1923–1948); British Railways (1948–closure)

Station closed	*Date of closure*
Sidley *	15 June 1964
Bexhill West **	15 June 1964

* Closed between 1 January 1917 and 14 June 1920.
** Originally named Bexhill until 1920 (it was closed between 1 January and 5 November 1917). Renamed Bexhill (Eastern) on 9 July 1923 and Bexhill West in November 1929.

Exterior of Sidley station, 26 October 1947.

Sidley Station, facing Crowhurst.

The Crowhurst, Sidley & Bexhill Railway Company was incorporated in 1897 and the line was approved on 15 July 1897; it opened in 1902. The line ran from the South Eastern Railway's Tonbridge to Hastings line across a broad valley and then down to the coastal suburbs of Bexhill. A spectacular sight on the route was the seventeen-arch viaduct across the Crowhurst Valley.

S.E.R. Station, Bexhill-on-Sea

Bexhill Station, 1906

The viaduct was built between 1897 and 1902 at a cost of £244,000. It was an impressive structure reaching a maximum height of 70 feet and each pier was built on concrete blocks measuring 54 x 32 feet, sunk approximately 30 feet into marshland. The viaduct was demolished in 1969 following the closure of the line in 1964. The line had been temporarily closed between 1 January 1917 and 1 March 1919.

Bexhill West Station, facing the dead end, 30 June 1956. Locomotive No. 31269 is at the head of a train.

The Dyke Railway and The Dyke Steep Grade Railway

Passenger service withdrawn   1 January 1939
Distance   3 ½ miles
Company   The Brighton & Dyke Railway (1877–1922);
Southern Railway (1923–1939)

Station closed	*Date of closure*
Rowan Halt *	1 January 1939
Golf Club Halt	1 January 1939
Dyke Station **	1 January 1939

* Opened on 18 December 1933 to serve the Aldrington Manor Estate.
** Terminus, located a quarter of a mile short of the summit of Devil's Dyke.

London, Brighton & South Coast Railway No. 168 at Dyke Station.

Dyke Station from the Down.

Authorised on 2 August 1877 and opening ten years later, the first train on the Dyke Railway ran on 1 September 1887. A splendid opening ceremony had been planned, but unfortunately the weather decided otherwise. A sumptuous luncheon had been prepared and music was to be provided by the 1st Sussex Artillery, but the heavy rain showed no let up. Eventually the luncheon party took pity on the band and invited them inside the marquee. The lunch was accompanied by entertaining speeches, and it was all over in time for the special guests to return to Brighton on the 5 p.m. train.

THE DYKE RAILWAY AND THE DYKE STEEP GRADE RAILWAY

Dyke Station, October 1933.

Upon opening, the branch line ran from West Brighton (now named Hove) direct to Dyke Station located at the foot of Devil's Dyke. Over the years the traffic on line lessened and to try and improve it further halts were opened. The line had a temporary closure during the First World War and finally ceased operation on 31 December 1938.

The Devil's Dyke is a 300 foot, dry V-shaped valley which forms part of the Southern England Chalk Formation. It is an historic beauty spot of the South Downs. In 1897 due to the growing number of tourists, a steep grade railway was built descending from the rim on the valley bowl. It was opened on 24 July 1897 and ran for a distance of 840 feet. The carriages ran on three-feet narrow gauge railway tracks. Due to a non-constant track gradient, the two cars had to run independently. The steep grade railway closed in 1908.

Kemp Town Branch

Passenger service withdrawn	2 January 1933
Distance	1 ¼ miles
Company	London, Brighton & South Coast Railway (1880–1922);
	Southern Railway (1923–1948); British Railways (1948–closure)

Station closed	*Date of closure*
Lewes Road Halt *	2 January 1933
Hartington Road Halt	1 June 1911
Kemp Town **	2 January 1933

* Originally named Lewes Road until closure on 1 January. Reopened and renamed on 10 August 1919.
** Closed between 1 January 1917 and 10 August 1919.

Lewes Road Halt facing Brighton, 23 June 1956.

LBSCR 0-4-2T No. 28 *Isfield* at Kemp Town Station.

This branch line diverged from the Brighton to Lewes line, east of Ditchling Road Tunnel. Authorised on 13 May 1864, it took five years to build and ran for most of its length either on an embankment or viaduct, and through a 946-yard tunnel before emerging at its terminus.

There were two viaducts on the line. The first was located over Lewes Road (fourteen-arch) and the second was located over Hartington Road (three-arch). The branch was intended to provide a suburban service for the east side of Brighton, but became an early casualty to competition from trams and buses.

Lewes — East Grinstead

Passenger service withdrawn	17 March 1958
Distance	17 miles
Company	Lewes & East Grinstead Railway (1877–1878);
	London, Brighton & South Coast Railway (1878–1922);
	Southern Railway (1923–1948); British Railways (1948–1958)

Stations closed	*Date of closure*
Barcombe *	13 June 1955
Newick & Chailey **	17 March 1958
Sheffield Park ***	17 March 1958
Horsted Keynes	28 October 1963
West Hoathly **	17 March 1958
Kingscote ****	17 March 1958

* Originally named New Barcombe until 1 January 1855. The last train was on 28 May 1955.

** Closed between 13 June 1955 and 7 August 1956.

*** Originally named Fletching & Sheffield Park until 1 January 1883. Closed between 13 June 1955 and 7 August 1956. Reopened on the preservation Bluebell Railway on 31 July 1960.

**** Originally named Kingscote for Turner's Hill. Closed between 13 June 1955 and 7 August 1956. Renamed and reopened on the preservation Bluebell Railway on 23 April 1994.

Horsted Keynes, West Hoathly and Kingscote are in the companion book *Lost Railways of West Sussex*.

Barcombe Station, 1930s.

LBSCR 0-4-2 No. 185 *George A. Wallis* at Barcombe Station, *c.* 1900.

Authorised on 10 August 1877 and opening on 1 August 1882, local school children were given the day off school to join the many who watched the first train. The line left the Lewes to Uckfield line at Culver Junction. Barcombe Station was opened as New Barcombe but changed name the following year.

LBSCR No. 373 at Barcombe Station.

The original Barcombe Station was located on the Uckfield line; when the East Grinstead line opened, its name was changed to Barcombe Mills Station. Barcombe village had a sparse population and yet was lucky enough to have two stations. There was a ten-arch viaduct known as the Imberhorne Viaduct, named after a nearby estate.

Newick & Chailey Station, *c.* 1900.

Sheffield Park Station, April 1931. No. 537 shunts a horse box from the 8.35 London Bridge – Brighton train.

No. 42080, at the head of the 8.03 from London Bridge to Brighton, takes on water at Sheffield Park, March 1954.

Lewes — Uckfield

Passenger service withdrawn 4 May 1969
Distance 8 ½ miles
Company Lewes & Uckfield Railway (1856–1859); London, Brighton & South Coast Railway (1878–1922);
Southern Railway (1923–1948); British Railways (1948–1958)

Stations closed	*Date of closure*
Barcombe Mills *	4 May 1969
Isfield	4 May 1969
Uckfield **	13 May 1991

* Originally named Barcombe until 1 January 1885.
** Replaced by the new Uckfield Station 50 metres north.

Barcombe Mills Station.

Authorised on 27 July 1856, this line was opened on 18 October 1858 by the Lewes & Uckfield Railway Company, which was taken over the following year by the London, Brighton & South Coast Railway.

Isfield Station, *c.* **1900.**

Barcombe Mills Station was originally known as Barcombe, but was changed to avoid confusion with the station of the same name on the Lewes to East Grinstead line. The station was situated nearly one mile to the southeast of Barcombe village in an area comprising a cluster of hamlets. Isfield Station received a great deal of traffic during the First World War. Milk churns were brought to Isfield by rail, as were German POWs who were brought in for forestry work in the Plashett Wood area. At the end of the day they were marched back to the station to board the train back to camp.

Uckfield Station.

The last train on the line ran on 23 February 1969 and bus replacement was provided by British Rail until the official closure on 6 May 1969. The line was earmarked for closure under the Beeching cuts; unsafe bridges on the approach to Lewes sealed the line's fate.

Exterior of Uckfield Station, 1900.

Polegate — Hailsham and Hailsham — Eridge: the 'Cuckoo Line'

Passenger service withdrawn   Polegate to Hailsham: 9 September 1968;
Hailsham to Eridge: 14 June 1965

Distance   20 ½ miles
Company   Tunbridge Wells & Eastbourne Railway (1846– 1876);
London, Brighton & South Coast Railway (1876–1922);
Southern Railway (1923–1948); British Railways (1948–closure)

Stations closed	*Date of closure*
Polegate *	25 May 1986
Hailsham	9 September 1968
Hellingly	14 June 1965
Horam **	14 June 1965

Stations closed	*Date of closure*
Heathfield & Cross In Hand	14 June 1965
Mayfield	14 June 1965
Rotherfield & Mark Cross ***	14 June 1965

* This replaced the first Polegate Station (275 metres west) on 3 October 1881. On the date of closure it was replaced by the reopened first station.

** Originally named Horeham Road for Waldron until renamed Horeham Road & Waldron on 1 June 1890. Renamed as Waldron & Horeham Road on 1 April 1900 and as Waldron & Horam on 1 January 1935 before being given its final name on 21 September 1953.

*** Originally named Rotherfield until 1 November 1901.

Polegate Station from the level crossing, *c.* 1910.

Polegate Station, October 1950.

This line was completed in two stages. The first section, owned by the Tunbridge Wells & Eastbourne Railway Company, opened from Polegate to Hailsham on 14 May 1849 (closing in 1968). The remainder of the line, Hailsham to Eridge, was completed and opened 31 years later in 1880 by the London, Brighton & South Coast Railway (closing in 1965).

Hailsham Station looking south, *c.* 1900.

Hailsham Station was a grand building with two substantial platforms, numerous sidings and also a private siding which served a brick works one and a half miles to the south of the village.

Disused station at Hailsham looking north towards the bridge, April 1972.

The station at Horam opened as Horeham Road for Waldron and was built to serve the village of Waldron two and a half miles away and the nearby Horeham Manor. The final name change to Horam came after the Second World War.

Hellingly Station. 687.

Hellingly Station from the bridge, *c.* 1900. Hellingly Hospital's wooden platform and electric overhead wires are on the left (see page 40).

At Heathfield there was a 270-yard tunnel which became famous for being the area where the country's first natural gas deposits were found in 1895. Mayfield was a little used station located a half mile from the village centre and there was a private siding which served a local milk depot. The siding closed in 1950.

Hellingly from the bridge, April 1972.

At Redgate Mill Junction the line joined with the Uckfield line. A single track ran parallel with the Uckfield line for one and a half miles towards Eridge. In 1894 this stretch was incorporated as a double track to allow easier use.

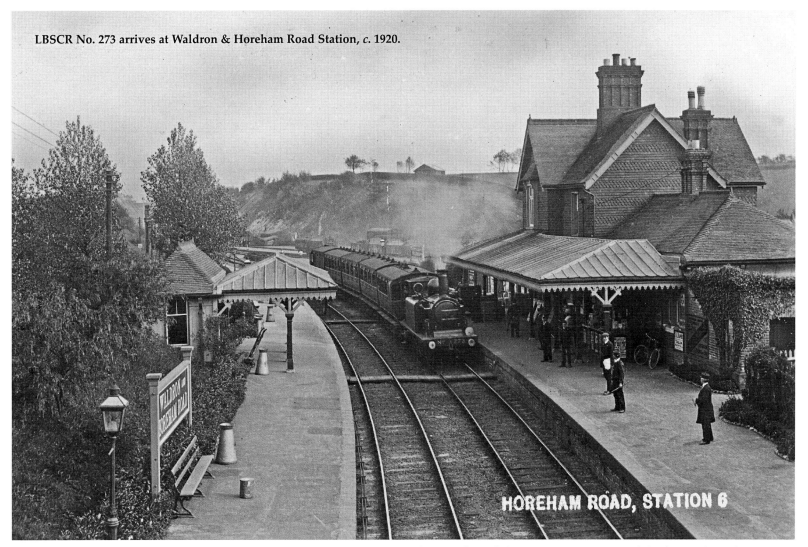

LBSCR No. 273 arrives at Waldron & Horeham Road Station, *c*. 1920.

HOREHAM ROAD, STATION 6

The name 'Cuckoo Line' was adopted by the railway men and relates to an old Sussex legend that every year on 14 April the first cuckoo of summer is released at the Heathfield Fair.

Heathfield Station, May 1948.

Heathfield Station, *c.* 1900.

HEATHFIELD STATION

Heathfield from the railway, 1905.

Heathfield from Railway

J.V.

Mayfield Station, 1905.

Mayfield Station, 1951.

Mayfield Station, April 1954.

Rotherfield & Mark Cross Station from the east, *c.* 1905.

Rotherfield & Mark Cross Station from the south, *c.* 1905.

Hellingly — Hellingly Hospital

Passenger service withdrawn   1931
Distance   1 ¼ miles
Company   East Sussex County Council

The only stops on this line were Farm and Park House sidings and the hospital itself.

Hellingly Station, shortly before the hospital line platform was removed.

To the south of Hellingly Station was a siding which led to the nearby 'mental hospital', as such establishments were known in those days. Opening in 1880, the siding had no connection with the London, Brighton & South Coast Railway except for a small wooden platform which was built opposite the station's main platform. The railway was used to transport building materials and stores to the hospital. Visitors and staff also used the line. In 1903 the line was electrified using the hospital's own generated current at 500 volts DC. The line closed to passenger traffic in 1931 with the platform being removed in 1932. The line was closed to goods traffic in March 1959 and a special train for enthusiasts ran that month.

Rother Valley Railway *

Passenger service withdrawn	4 January 1954
Distance	21 ½ miles
Company	The Rother Valley (Light) Railway (1896–1904);
	The Kent & East Sussex Light Railway (1904–1948);
	British Railways (1948–closure)

Stations closed	*Date of closure*
Robertsbridge	4 January 1954
Salehurst Halt	4 January 1954
Junction Road	4 January 1954

Stations closed	*Date of closure*
Bodiam **	4 January 1954
Northiam **	4 January 1954
Wittersham Road **	4 January 1954

* Closed stations on this line that were in Kent were Rolvenden, Tenterden Town, Tenterden St Michaels, High Halden Road, Biddenden, Frittenden Road and Headcorn. In 1904 the railway changed its name to the Kent and East Sussex Light Railway

** Reopened by Tenterden Railway Company Ltd: Wittersham Road in 1977, Northiam in 1990 and Bodiam in 2000.

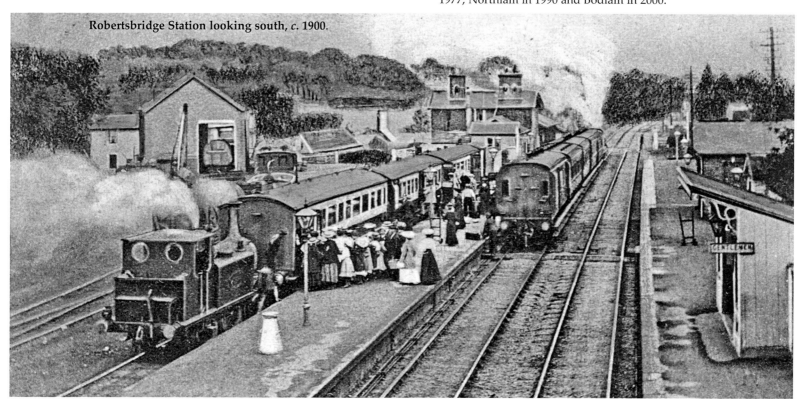

Robertsbridge Station looking south, *c.* 1900.

Robertsbridge Station, looking north towards Tunbridge Wells, April 1947.

Authorised in 1896, this line was opened in sections: Robertsbridge to Rolvenden in 1900; Rolvenden to Tenterden Town in 1903; and Tenterden Town to Headcorn in 1905. The line started from a short bay at the London end of the down platform at Robertsbridge and followed the Rother Valley; this meant that the line had to be built high enough to avoid flooding.

Salehurst Halt, January 1954. The halt was provided in 1929 at the request of the vicar of Salehurst to provide a convenient stop for his congregation.

In 1916 the track flooded and also moved due to the pressure. The situation was only discovered when the engine pulling the first train of the day derailed and came to rest on its side against a willow tree.

A very busy Bodiam Station. The photograph is thought to have been taken on the official opening day of the station.

The line was expected to produce a good level of income due to monthly markets being held in Robertsbridge, two large flour mills served by special sidings and a thriving farming community along the route. Hop growing was also a strong feature of the area. The line was affectionately known as 'the Farmers' Line' and occasionally as 'the Hoppers' Line' due to the fact it served hordes of Londoners who descended on Kent for the annual hop-picking. However, by the late 1930s the line was falling into decline.

Bodiam Station looking west as KESLR No. 9 arrives with the 12.55 Robertsbridge to Tenterden service, March 1931.

The Second World War helped the line regain some of its importance as it became a secondary route towards the coast when the main lines were hit by German bombs. The last passenger train ran in January 1954, although the goods traffic from Robertsbridge to Tenterden continued to run until 1961. During this time a number of hop pickers' trains used the line and four specials were organised, one by the Branch Line Society, one by the Ramblers' Association, and two by the Locomotive Club of Great Britain.

In 1974 the Kent & East Sussex Railway Preservation Society (later renamed the Tenterden Railway Company Ltd) was created and reopened a section of track from Tenterden Town to Rolvenden. By 1990 Northiam Station was reopened and in April 2000 trains reached Bodiam, exactly 100 years after the line had opened.

Rye & Camber Tramway

Passenger service withdrawn	September 1939
Distance	1 ¾ miles
Company	Rye & Camber Tramway

Stations closed	*Date of closure*
Rye	September 1939
Gof Links Halt	September 1939
Camber Sands	September 1931

Victoria waits with a train at Rye Station, April 1909.

Camber with a train at Rye Station.

The tramway was constructed between January and July 1895. It connected Rye to the coast, ran for one and three-quarter miles and had three stations. The line was constructed entirely on private land and was the first to be designed by consulting engineer Holman F. Stephens.

Golf Links Halt.

The line was initially built to transport golfers to the Rye Golf Club; however in 1908 an extension was built to Camber Sands. At the end of 1938 the terminal at Camber Sands was moved to a more accessible site and a tea room was added, but due to the outbreak of the Second World War this was only used for a short time.

After the initial success of the line, competition from car and bus transport brought the line into decline. Passenger services ended at the start of the war; however the line was still used by the government to transport parts for the PLUTO (Pipe Line under the Ocean) project. As a result of this, a special siding leading down to a new pier near Golf Links Halt was built by Canadian troops.

Camber Sands Halt.

Camber Sands Station, Rye and Camber Tramway.

By the end of the war the line was in such a run-down condition it was decided that it was beyond repair and in 1947 it was sold for scrap. In February 1949 the Rye and Camber Tramways Company Ltd was liquidated.

Three Bridges — Tunbridge Wells West *

Passenger service withdrawn	8 July 1985
Distance	20 miles
Company	East Grinstead, Groombridge &
	Tunbridge Wells Railway (1862–1864);
	London, Brighton & South Coast Railway (1864–1922);
	Southern Railway (1923–1948);
	British Railways (1948–1985)

Stations closed	*Date of closure*
Rowfant	2 January 1967
Grange Road	2 January 1967

Stations closed	*Date of closure*
East Grinstead High Level	2 January 1967
Forest Row	2 January 1967
Hartfield	2 January 1967
Withyham	2 January 1967
Groombridge	8 July 1985

* The section from Rowfant to East Grinstead is in the companion book *Lost Railways of West Sussex*.

** The closed station on this line that was in Kent was High Rocks Halt.

Forest Row facing Tunbridge Wells, May 1962.

Hartfield Station, September 1912.

The Station, Hartfield.

The first East Grinstead station was opened in 1855 with the completion of the line from Three Bridges. When the line was extended to Tunbridge Wells in 1866 the station was moved a few yards to the north. Then, when the line from Lewes was opened on 1 August 1882, the station was again relocated, this time some distance to the west; however, as this new station was not complete, all trains between Three Bridges and Tunbridge Wells used the 1866 station. The new high level station opened on 15 October 1883, at which time the previous station was closed (it was demolished in February 1908).

Withyham Station, April 1954.

The new station was arranged on two levels. The higher level was equipped with two island platforms serving four tracks on the Three Bridges line. The lower level had a double-line, two-platform station to serve the line from Lewes. The high level station closed on 2 January 1967. In February 1970 British Railways carried out a remodelling of the low level station, replacing the old station building with a more modern, small building which reflected its new status as the terminus of a branch line from Oxford. The line is still in use today and has two trains per hour to London Victoria.

Groombridge Station, March 1948.

The line from East Grinstead to Tunbridge Wells West was opened in 1866 by the London, Brighton & South Coast Railway. Construction had been started by the East Grinstead, Groombridge & Tunbridge Wells Railway Company, which was taken over by the larger company in 1864. The line was closed between Three Bridges and Groombridge in 1967, the remainder to Tunbridge Wells remaining open until 1985.

Stations closed on lines still open to passengers: Hastings & St Leonards Line

Stations closed
West Marina Station

Date of closure
1967

West Marina Station looking east, March 1956.

St Leonards West Marina Station looking west, 1931.

Postscript: The Lines That Never Were

The Ouse Valley Railway was approved in 1864, with work commencing in 1865. The route was to take the line from south of Balcombe along the Ouse Valley to Uckfield and then southeast to Hailsham where the line would have connected with the 1849 Polegate line. The idea behind the line was purely political and traffic would have been minimal. An armistice between the South Eastern Railway, the London, Chatham & Dover Railway and the London, Brighton & South Coast Railway in 1866 brought the work on the line to an end; in fact, no track was ever laid along the route.

As well as the Ouse Valley Railway there were numerous other lines that were authorised, but never actually constructed: Brighton – Rottingdean – Newhaven Direct (authorised 1886); Eastbourne – Seaford – Newhaven (authorised 1889); and Bexhill – Rotherfield (authorised 1899).